A BANTAM PATHFINDER EDITION

SO-CPS-862

The key to writing about people is understanding their character. **AN EYE FOR PEOPLE** contains over 150 photographs, paintings, sculptures and cartoons with examples from Cartier-Bresson, Picasso, Moore and Peanuts. William Faulkner, Dorothy Parker, Ernest Hemingway and Joseph Heller provide examples of written work. **AN EYE FOR PEOPLE** is the answer for those who wish to be articulate at all levels of writing.

Learn to analyze people in an entirely fresh and unique way.

**AN EYE FOR PEOPLE:
A WRITER'S GUIDE TO CHARACTER**
by Hart Day Leavitt

Bantam Books in the Stop, Look & Write Series

STOP, LOOK, AND WRITE!
PICTURES FOR WRITING
THE WRITER'S EYE
AN EYE FOR PEOPLE: A WRITER'S GUIDE TO CHARACTER

An Eye for People:

A Writer's Guide to Character

BY HART DAY LEAVITT

BANTAM PATHFINDER EDITIONS
TORONTO / NEW YORK / LONDON

A NATIONAL GENERAL COMPANY

AN EYE FOR PEOPLE: A WRITER'S GUIDE TO CHARACTER
A Bantam Pathfinder Book / published October 1970

ACKNOWLEDGMENTS

Excerpt from Salinger: A Critical and Personal Portrait, *edited and introduced by Henry Anatole Grunwald. Copyright © 1962 by Henry Grunwald. Reprinted by permission of Harper & Row, Publishers, Inc. and Harold Matson Co., Inc. Excerpt from "The Three Day Blow," by Ernest Hemingway. From his* In Our Time. *Copyright 1925 by Charles Scribner's Sons; renewed 1953 by Ernest Hemingway. Reprinted by permission of Charles Scribner's Sons and Jonathan Cape, Ltd. Excerpt from "The Oedipus Complex," by Frank O'Connor. From* The Collected Stories of Frank O'Connor. *Copyright 1950 by Frank O'Connor. Reprinted by permission of Alfred A. Knopf, Inc. and A. D. Peters & Co. Excerpt from* A Streetcar Named Desire *by Tennessee Williams. Copyright 1947 by Tennessee Williams. Reprinted by permission of New Directions Publishing Corporation and Elaine Greene, Ltd. Excerpt from* American Painting in the Twentieth Century *by Henry Geldzahler. Copyright © 1965 by The Metropolitan Museum of Art and reprinted with their permission. Excerpt from* Michelangelo *by Romain Rolland. Copyright © 1962 by Crowell Collier Publishing Company. Reprinted by permission of The Macmillan Company. Excerpt from* Art Through the Ages *by Helen Gardiner. Copyright 1926, 1936, 1948, © 1954, 1959, 1964 by Harcourt, Brace & World, Inc. and reprinted with their permission. Excerpt from "Enroute with Robert F. Kennedy," by The Associated Press. Copyright © 1968 by The Associated Press and reprinted with their permission. Excerpt from* Portrait of the Artist as a Young Man *by James Joyce. Copyright 1916 by B. W. Huebsch, renewed 1944 by Nora Joyce. Reprinted by permission of The Viking Press, Inc. and Jonathan Cape, Ltd. Excerpt from* A Companion Guide to Rome *by Georgina Masson. Copyright © 1965 by Harper & Row, Publishers, Inc. and reprinted with their permission and that of Collins Publishers. Excerpt from* Catch-22 *by Joseph Heller. Copyright © 1955 by Joseph Heller. Reprinted by permission of Simon & Schuster, Inc. and Jonathan Cape, Ltd. Excerpt from "Graven Image," by John O'Hara. From* Selected Short Stories of John O'Hara. *Copyright © 1956 by Random House, Inc. and reprinted with their permission and that of John O'Hara. Excerpt from* The Great Gatsby *by F. Scott Fitzgerald. Copyright 1925 by Charles Scribner's Sons; renewed 1953 by Frances Scott Fitzgerald Lanahan. Reprinted by permission of Charles Scribner's Sons and The Bodley Head, Ltd. Excerpt from* A Separate Peace *by John Knowles. Copyright © 1959 by John Knowles. Reprinted by permission of The Macmillan Company and Secker & Warburg, Ltd. Excerpt from "The Door," by E. B. White. From his* The Second Tree from the Corner. *Copyright 1939, © 1967 by E. B. White. Reprinted by permission of Harper & Row, Publishers, Inc. and Hamish Hamilton, Ltd. "Boy With Frogs," by Sy Kahn. Copyright © 1963 by Sy Kahn and reprinted with his permission. Excerpt from "The Use of Force," by William Carlos Williams. From his* The Farmer's Daughters. *Copyright 1938 by William Carlos Williams. Reprinted by permission of New Directions Publishing Corporation. Excerpt from* Luv *by Murray Schisgal. Copyright © 1963, 1965 by Murray Schisgal. Reprinted by permission of Coward-McCann, Inc. and International Famous Agency.*

Published simultaneouly in the United States and Canada

---

*Bantam Books are published by Bantam Books, Inc., a National
General company. Its trade-mark, consisting of the words "Bantam
Books" and the portrayal of a bantam, is registered in the United
States Patent Office and in other countries. Marcia Registrada.
Bantam Books, Inc., 666 Fifth Avenue, New York, N.Y. 10019*

PRINTED IN THE UNITED STATES OF AMERICA

Contents

Introduction

What is character?

How can it be discovered, so that you can observe it, talk about it, and write about it?

First, study a person's *appearance:* size, actions, colors, manners, expressions, and clothes—the physical evidence. If you see these outward signs accurately and completely, you can write so that your audience sees the person as a distinct individual, unlike others who may resemble him. This visual identification is important, since your reader may not have the slightest idea whom you're talking about.

> Michael Lowes hummed as he shaved, amused by the face he saw—the pallid, asymmetrical face, with the right eye so much higher than the left, and its eyebrow so peculiarly arched, like a "v" turned upside down.—Conrad Aiken, "The Impulse"

In such exact writing, precise characteristics of a particular individual are expressed in specific, visual language so that the reader can almost see what the words say, words like "asymmetrical," "arched," "upside down."

If you look at someone sloppily, incompletely, or tritely, you simply cannot write like this. What will appear instead is a dull picture without detail, or a fuzzy focus on the details you do mention. There will be almost no characterization, as in the following from an amateur story:

> The captain was a pretty big guy, and when he came out on the field, all the girls looked at him.

These two quotes reveal an important connection between purpose and language. Maybe the amateur description is poor because of a poor vocabulary—words like "big," "pretty," and "looked"—but the fault is more likely to be an unclear purpose, which is always the result of careless observation and thought. In actual life, for example, those girls did not just LOOK at the captain; they watched him in a very special way, and that is what would reveal their character.

A second vital element of character is what might be called the *temper of emotion.* For this, you must also notice the physical signs, and if you describe the right ones precisely, you will reveal just how much a character feels.

> The boy, crouching, small for his age, small and wiry like his father, in patched and faded jeans even too small for him, with straight, uncombed, brown hair and eyes gray and wild as storm scud, saw the men between him and the table part and become a lane of grim faces, at the end of which he saw the Justice, a shabby, collarless, graying man in spectacles, beckoning him.—William Faulkner, "Barn Burning"

The depth of this boy's fear comes out in words like "crouching," "gray and wild," and "grim faces."

Often, however, emotion is a subtler element than any literal appearance can indicate, and you must try to discover what lies behind the visible manifestations. A slap in the face may appear to suggest an angry temperament, but may mean something quite different. A kiss may look like affection, but have a different meaning.

In such moments, the truth may be discovered through a search for relationships: how do actions, words, and feeling relate, especially in terms of cause and effect? Look for comparisons and contrasts between what you can see is actually true, and what you imagine MAY be true. By this effort you may develop the habit of making pieces of life fit together, not only while you are observing but while thinking and writing. Your words and ideas may speak more forcefully through symbols, metaphors and other images that create connections.

In the following passage, though something of the girls' emotion is revealed in the opening lines, the dramatic essence appears at the end:

Now, as they walked across to Fifth Avenue, with their skirts swirled by the hot wind, they received audible admiration. Young men grouped lethargically about newsstands awarded them murmurs, exclamations, even, the ultimate tribute—whistles. Annabel and Midge passed without the condescension of hurrying their pace; they held their heads higher and set their feet with exquisite precision, as if they stepped over the necks of peasants.—Dorothy Parker, "The Standard of Living"

Apparently, for Miss Parker, it was not enough to say merely that these girls felt superior. She wanted to expose the degree, the height, of their conceit, and so she measured it in relation to peasants.

Notice how the intensity of a somewhat different feeling is dramatized by the precise particulars following the general term for the emotion experienced—astonishment:

"Not so fast! You're driving too fast!" said Mrs. Mitty. "What are you driving so fast for?"

"Hmmm?" said Walter Mitty. He looked at his wife, in the seat beside him, with shocked astonishment. She seemed grossly unfamiliar, like a strange woman who had yelled at him from the crowd.—James Thurber, "The Secret Life of Walter Mitty"

There are many things in this life which can shock and astonish a man, but the emotion takes on the defined form of a peculiar distaste when it associates one's lawful wedded wife with a strange woman yelling out of a crowd.

A third element of character is *motivation*, which, although related to temper and emotion, is more complicated and more private. An understanding of emotion is often only a first step toward the discovery of motive. Though Dorothy Parker indicates intense boredom in Annabel and Midge, she tells nothing of WHY the girls are bored.

To discover motives and write effectively about them requires the most thorough and imaginative observation of individual behavior and feelings, and a constant comparing of characters, including one's own. This means studying those peculiar actions and words that are repeated over and over again. A brief look-see tells almost nothing.

It will be particularly difficult to find motives when all you see is one picture, and no one should be expected to PROVE a point, as in mathematics. But by studying and comparing every detail, and by making educated guesses, you may come close; if you can produce discerning evidence, you may be very convincing. Look especially for what may be unguarded gestures and expressions, for they are the ones that usually suggest the true motives. Always ask the question: what does he really want? That is the essence of motivation.

One way to write about motives is direct psychological analysis, using language that cites the reasons, as in this passage.

The hero of *The Catcher in the Rye* is usually described as a rebel, either against the materialism and ugliness of "our society," or against the realities of the adult world. But he does not make a very satisfactory rebel because he is not FOR anything. Everybody knows that the well-adjusted, successful "adult" rebel should have a positive program; otherwise, after all, is he not merely an anarchist? Among the critics who know that Holden lacks a positive program is Phoebe Caulfield, his sister, who complains that he doesn't like ANYthing that is happening.—Henry Grunwald, *Salinger: A Critical and Personal Portrait*

This is the expository approach which, if done well, is perfectly satisfactory.

But there is another method, the method of the artist and creator rather than the analyst. Here motives are suggested by careful choice of dialogue and careful placement of these choices so that they produce a chemical reaction in the reader.

In the following passage from Ernest Hemingway's story "The Three Day Blow," it is interesting to speculate why both speakers subtly shift the emphasis in the last three lines of dialogue. No definite answer is given, but possible motives can be discovered by connecting these lines with what goes before, and the silence at the end.

"How is your Dad?" Nick asked respectfully.

"He's all right," Bill said. "He gets a little wild sometimes."

"He's a swell guy," Nick said. He poured water into his glass out of the pitcher. It mixed slowly with the whiskey. There was more whiskey than water.

"You bet your life he is," Bill said.

"My old man's all right," Nick said.

"You're damn right he is," said Bill.

"He claims he's never taken a drink in his life," Nick said, as though announcing a scientific fact.

"Well, he's a doctor. My old man's a painter. That's different."

"He's missed a lot," Nick said sadly.

"You can't tell," Bill said. "Everything's got its compensations."

"He says he's missed a lot himself," Nick confessed.

"Well, Dad's had a tough time," Bill said.

"It all evens up," Nick said.

They sat looking into the fire and thinking of this profound truth.

Another way to communicate motivation is to arrange the carefully chosen details of action so that they suggest a personal cause. A boy's reasons are hinted at in this passage from a story by Frank O'Connor, just after the boy's father has come home from the Army:

The day when Father came in to dinner, he took off his boots and put on his slippers, donned a dirty old cap and began to talk gravely to Mother, who looked anxious. Naturally, I disliked her looking anxious, because it destroyed her good looks, so I interrupted him.

"Just a moment, Larry!" she said gently.

This was only what she said when we had boring visitors, so I attached no importance to it and went on talking.

"Do be quiet, Larry!" she said impatiently. "Don't you hear me talking to Daddy?"

This was the first time I had heard those ominous words, "talking to Daddy," and I couldn't help feeling that if this was how God answered prayers, he couldn't listen to them very attentively.

"Why are you talking to Daddy?" I asked with as great a show of indifference as I could muster.

—Frank O'Connor, "My Oedipus Complex"

Very often and most unfortunately, writing about character produces a kind of hot-air prose which either tells the reader nothing, or misleads him with mindless generalizations. It is written by both amateurs and professionals, and is especially beloved of some students, Boy Scout leaders, and writers of personnel reports; it is also the foundation of gossip. Technically it is known as *abstract generalizing,* and it comes from a way of seeing, thinking and writing that is the exact opposite of the passage just quoted. It is not specific, or original; it is expository and moral. It deals with undigested ideas and, in both conversation and writing, takes up more time and space than all other methods of characterization. Unhappily, it is the easiest, since it requires almost no observation and no thought. You just turn on the handiest faucet:

> He's the stupidest character you ever saw. He doesn't have a brain in his head. You ought to hear the silly things he says. Anybody who acts the way he does should have his head examined.

Or:

> We have always found Alice to be a very good person. She is reliable and apparently was brought up in a fine way. We are especially impressed with her attitude toward those older than she is. It really is quite remarkable in this day and age. We think she is a very good candidate.

You can write stuff like this almost without looking at the person, or the image. In fact, words like "stupidest" and "a fine way" can easily be written about people you don't even know.

One of the best ways to cure excessive and platitudinous generalizing is to balance the big abstract words with precise, sensuous ones:

> His own life had been a gray one, from temperament rather than circumstance, and he had been drawn to his new wife by the unperturbed gaiety which kept her fresh and elastic at an age when most women's activities are growing slack.—Edith Wharton, *The Other Two*

One reason this is good writing about character is that the valid but incomplete generalizations, like "circumstance," "age," and "activities" are sharpened and developed by the more vivid words "elastic," "gray," and "slack." Instead of "gray," for example, a less perceptive writer might have written "plain," or "uninteresting," and let it go at that.

One final and rather special problem about observing and describing character, whether in real life or art, involves the elusive distinction between character and personality. Many times, as some illustrations in this book suggest, the two are in sharp contrast. "Personality" is more immediately revealed and its cultivation often more fun, as in the modern fad of "Personality Posters." It is usually caught by a single colorful habit which stops the eye and makes an entertaining picture. Hundreds of professional performers make their living out of a gesture, a look, a sound, or a manner of dress; deliberate tricks that sometimes have little to do with underlying character, as the public may discover to its disillusionment. Character runs deep, often hidden at first sight; it is born in a man and developed by years of environment, circumstances, and experience.

To write well, it is necessary to learn all you can about character and personality, since they form the most important elements in both creative writing and impersonal exposition. Novels, plays, short stories, character sketches, personality profiles, admissions applications, personnel reports, job references—all are good or bad according to their clarity, accuracy, and depth of characterization.

Students can take courses in psychology or the behavioral sciences and learn much about character. But there are many opportunities to learn even more by watching people—as they act themselves, or pretend to be someone else, or try to reveal nothing. Every good writer, like every good painter and photographer, is a perceptive observer, and has a good time at it too. He learns to know what expressions, gestures, and movements of the body mean. He also learns to reject what is unimportant.

This book is a visual study of humanity, designed to show you how and where to find subject matter for characterization. It will present paintings, photographs, sculpture, cartoons, and other images as revelations of character. Like other books in the *STOP, LOOK and WRITE* series, written exercises will be suggested, both about the images and about their relationships to actual life. As an added feature, there are examples of the best characterizations from old and modern literature.

Before writing about any image, it is urged that students first study everything in the whole section.

Part I

Images
With
Interpretations

The following passages illustrate the three elements of characterization—appearance, temper, and motivation— and dramatize how they work together to reveal accurate and imaginative pictures of human nature. Identify the italicized elements and then look for others. Which are the most powerful and informative?

Blanche looks at a slip of paper, then at the building, then again at the slip and again at the building. Her expression is one of *shocked* disbelief at the poverty and atmosphere of decay. Her appearance is incongruous to this setting. She is daintily dressed in a white suit with a *fluffy bodice,* necklace and earrings of pearl, white gloves and hat, looking as if she were arriving at a summer tea or cocktail party in the garden district. She is of a delicate beauty that must *avoid a strong light.* There is something about her uncertain manner, as well as her white clothes, that suggests a moth.—Tennessee Williams, Stage directions for *A Streetcar Named Desire*

Jack talks *loud and hard* all the time, and if anybody manages to get a word in, he just waits, with his eyes glazed, until HE can start up again. Sometimes he goes on with the same sentence ten minutes later, as if God had asked him what he meant. Many people think he's funny, but he really has *no sense of humor at all.* He makes a *noise like a laugh* but the rest of his face is set and fierce. He never laughs when anybody else does.—School character report on a student

When you have analyzed these quotations, study the images that follow. Each one is accompanied by a published characterization of the person represented. Compare images and language to see where the writers have expressed the major elements of characterization.

The Peasant—Antonello da Messina

The artist's most brilliant stroke has been almost entirely to hide the brow under the dark hat, thus centering attention on the eyes, nose and mouth. But this barbarously low brow, which robs the head of intelligence, appears contradicted by the sharp expression of the eyes, which, peering obliquely, reveal a malicious glint. The nose and mouth reaffirm coarseness and stupidity; but the smiling lips once again portray a contradiction, for they lack the eyes' purposeful intent. This subtle balancing of opposites . . . uncovers the conflicting elements in a peasant's face: sensuousness and simplicity, laughter and robust self-interest.—Vincent Cronin, *The Golden Honeycomb*

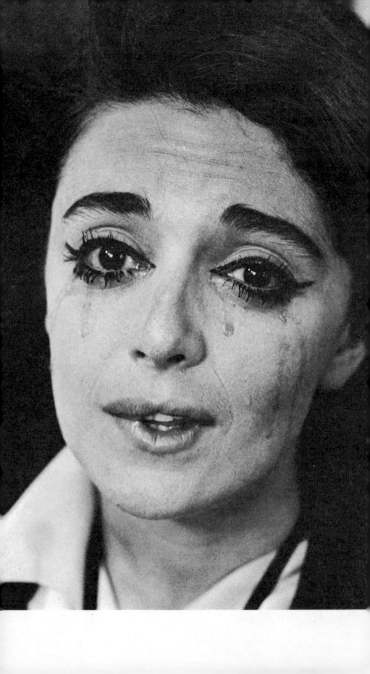

A human being changes continuously. His thoughts and moods change; his expressions and even his features change. Of a piece of sculpture you can produce identical pictures on two different days. But you cannot do it with a live human being.

If the human likeness consists of an infinite number of different images, which one should we try to capture? The most important one—namely, the image which reveals most completely the exterior and the interior of the subject. Such a picture is a portrait. A true portrait should be the testimony of how this person looked and what kind of human being he or she was.

You can study a famous painting, like, for instance, the "Mona Lisa," over and over again because there is so much in it. Her expression is such that on different days it will mean different things to you. This is the essence of a work of art; you don't touch bottom. If a picture has exactly the same meaning for everybody, it is a platitude and is meaningless as a work of art. The same is true of a portrait. If it is not rich in character and meaning, it is a poor portrait.

When I photograph a person I feel that I have the right to use any trick or mannerism. But then I don't have the right to call the result a portrait. Only when a photograph has truth, beauty and emotional impact can it be a great human document.

My picture of Anna-Maria Alberghetti on the opposite page is a "non-portrait" which captures an unusual expression but not the essence of the character.—Philippe Halsman, *Character in Photography*

Government Bureau—George Tooker

George Tooker has painted some of the most ominous of American surrealist pictures. We have the artist's word that the impulse for his "Government Bureau" came from his knowledge of Brooklyn's Municipal Building. The theme is the facelessness—the loss of individuality and will—of modern man when confronted with bureaucracy, the order to which he must submit and over which he has no control. A man-made system that dehumanizes man; this is Tooker's paradox. The structure of his painting, like the architecture it depicts, is cool and repetitive, reinforcing the theme of distance and isolation.—Henry Geldzahler, *American Painting in the Twentieth Century*

Moses—Michelangelo

24

Michelangelo's "Moses" is a supernatural and savage apparition half beast, half god. Pagan? Christian? No one knows. Two horns pierce the narrow skull, a flowing beard descends from his face to his knees like a parasitical vine attached to a great tree. He seems calm, but in his terrible jaw with close-shut teeth and projecting lower lip is wrath which shatters and crushes like the first chords of the overture to "Coriolanus." An implacable and murderous force, a tumult of rage and contempt wars in the silence of that arrogant being, with his huge bulk, his knotted arms—less brutal than those of most of Michelangelo's heroes, and with strong and beautiful hands—and left leg bent ready to rise. The dress is a barbarous one. No other work of Michelangelo is as completely finished. We feel that he had lived with it more than thirty years without being willing to let it go. He could see himself in it as in a superb mirror which gave him back the image that he had divined of his own soul. For the Moses is not only the most perfect artistic expression of his genius, but also its highest moral expression. Nowhere else has he so completely realized the majestic balance of a violent and passionate soul controlled by an iron will. Everywhere else passion is let loose and the human being is given into its hands. Here the savage elements are in suspense, ready to fuse. It is a thunder-cloud charged with lightning—Romain Rolland, *Michelangelo*

Beatrice Cenci—Guido Reni

There is a fixed and pale composure upon the features;
she seems sad and stricken down in spirit, yet the
despair thus expressed is lightened by the patience of
gentleness. Her head is bound with folds of white
drapery from which the yellow strings of her golden
hair escape, and fall about her neck. The moulding of
her face is exquisitely delicate; the eyebrows are distinct and arched; the lips have that permanent meaning
of imagination and sensibility which suffering has not
repressed. . . . In the whole mien there is a simplicity
and dignity which, united with her exquisite loveliness
and deep sorrow, is inexpressably pathetic.—Percy
Bysshe Shelley, Preface to *The Cenci*

American Gothic—Grant Wood

This famous painting has been interpreted in two entirely different ways. The artist himself imagined the Iowa farmer and his wife, standing before their stark neo-Gothic farmhouse, as the embodiment of narrow prejudice and self-righteous morality. Many viewers, however, completely missed the satirical intent, and praised the couple instead as symbols of American virtue and self-reliance.—Helen Gardiner, *Art through the Ages*

Summary

The interpretations you have just studied re-emphasize the kinds of observation and writing illustrated in the Introduction and on page 18.

The precision of Williams' "white suit with a fluffy bodice" is parallel to the specific description of the hat of Da Messina's peasant, or the head of Michelangelo's Moses.

In his analysis of the peasant's eyes the writer has expressed feeling with the same strong language used about the student's selfishness in the second example in this chapter.

For the power of analogy, notice how the temper of Moses is expressed in terms of thunder and lightning, just as the opposite feeling in Blanche is conveyed by the associations with a summer tea party.

The motivation behind the strange figures in Tooker's painting on page 22 is expressed in general, analytical language much like that in the student's character report. "A man-made system that dehumanizes man" is equivalent to "Many people think he's funny."

Almost every passage reflects the balance between generalization and precise, sensuous language referred to in the Introduction: Shelley characterizes with abstractions like "patience," "imagination," and "simplicity," but he also describes the girl's face with concrete images like "arched," and her clothes with "folds of white drapery."

Finally, a specific illustration of the difference between character and personality is revealed in Halsmann's comment about his non-portrait of Maria Alberghetti.

All of these interpretations provide models for your compositions about the images in the next chapter: models of perceptive observation, careful thoughts, and persuasive writing.

Images
with
no
Explanation

Accompanying the first two images are examples of bad writing: characterizations based on trite or sloppy observation and thought.

The other images appear alone, giving you the first chance to hunt for evidence of character on your own.

After studying the images, try writing the following: 1. Straight physical description, as if you were identifying the subject for someone who has not seen the picture. 2. A dramatic one-line summary of one aspect of character. 3. An imaginative interpretation of what the people might be thinking, what their personal style could be, and what they might be like to talk to.

Avoid excessive generalizing: using words like "way," "type," and "trait." Name the trait, and mention observable details which confirm the term. Also, try characterizing indirectly, symbolically, by organizing details to stand for ideas, ideas that are not mentioned.

. . . as I kissed her I would see the plucked accuracy of the eyebrow, the delicate lines at the corner of the eye toward me, and note the crinkled silky, shadowed texture of the eyelid, which could flicker sharply over the blue eyes. The eye, very slightly protruding, would be fixed glitteringly on some point beyond me.—Robert Penn Warren, *All the King's Men*

Before you write, study the particular image in relation to others, either in this book or in other publications. Or, relate the image to what you know about actual people. Like all other kinds of writing, characterization may be more emphatic through similarity and contrast.

Also, try imitating the kind of material developed by the perceptive journalist in his study of a famous and tragic political figure, Robert F. Kennedy, as quoted on page 36.

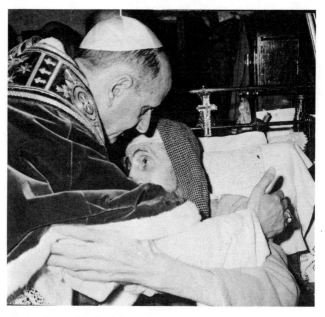

Examples of bad writing:
I guess that's the Pope and he's got his arms around some old woman.
It's a very sad picture.
Looks like Catholic propaganda to me.
The expression on the priest's face makes him appear as if he's just going through the motions.

Examples of bad writing:
This is a poor family.
Their faces show no feeling at all.
Man, that's a sad and worried group.
The Negro father is standing behind the white mother.

Lucrezia Panciatichi—Angnolo Bronzino

Self-Portrait—Albrecht Dürer

Enroute with Robert F. Kennedy, May 22 (A.P.)—
Now, at the airport, he moves through the last
crowd of the day, and the pushing and screaming
and grabbing are like they were at the super-
markets and the courthouse steps, and the schools.
Now, after midnight, he moves through the last
crowd with his glazed crowd-look, seeing no one,
his hands dipping into the pleading hands of
strangers, his body grabbed and tugged and be-
seeched by strangers, a small set smile protecting
the private little island no one reaches, hiding his
distaste for the scenes he invites.

Now, one more little speech, his tenth of the day:
the set jokes delivered with the deliberate timing
of a Las Vegas comic, the last familiar appeal—
"Give me your help"—the last embarrassed wave,
a limp dipping of the hand as if shaking water off
his fingers.

And finally the last push up to the plane, up the
ramp, up to the forward cabin, and the plane
roars down the runway, leaving Gary—or is it
Sioux Falls, or Fargo?—heading off to another day
and another blur . . .

Now almost alone at last, quiet at last, the glazed
look begins to dissolve, and he stares straight
ahead, beyond all other things in sight and there
comes then into those blue eyes, like a shadow
over a turquoise sea, a look of such infinite sad-
ness, or such terrible hurt, one feels compelled to
look away from the taut, angular face of Robert
Kennedy, candidate for President of the United
States.

All of the best elements of observation and character
ization appear in this perceptive reporter's picture
clear revelation of appearance in words like "taut, an
gular face;" dramatic expression of feeling in almo
every image of the second paragraph; and a direc
statement of motive in "hiding his distaste for th
scenes he invites."

One
Striking
Effect

In these images, character is revealed by *one* aspect of the visual impression. It may be a precise and limited detail, like the eyes or hands; or it may be a startling relationship between two people.

In some pictures there is little else to see but this one effect, and you can concentrate on what it means and how to communicate it. In others, the artist has included subordinate elements which help emphasize the major characteristic. One assignment is to explain how these minor parts contribute to the essence of the image. In the first picture, what is added by all the impersonal objects—the boxes, the paper, the jewelry?

Some of these dramatic, isolated moments may seem so clear that they do not challenge your understanding. You may be justified; but try conveying the obvious meaning to someone who has not seen the image, or who is not much interested in human nature.

Try a surprise in language, stressing the essential meaning in a different and perhaps memorable way. To avoid triteness, follow Robert Frost's advice: use common words in uncommon ways:

He was the kind of character who liked to have a loud time.

It may be that one peculiar detail can best be expressed through comparison, either simile or metaphor:

The policeman (on page 46) looks like a chipmunk who is afraid someone is going to steal his acorns.

Throughout this chapter, your problem as a student writer is not necessarily length of development, as it will be later. It is brevity, accuracy, and suggestiveness. It is the choice of an important single effect in the picture, and the right words to reveal it to someone else.

Celestine—Pablo Picasso

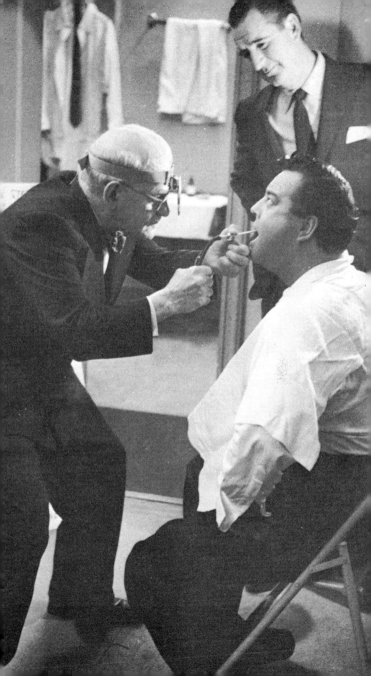

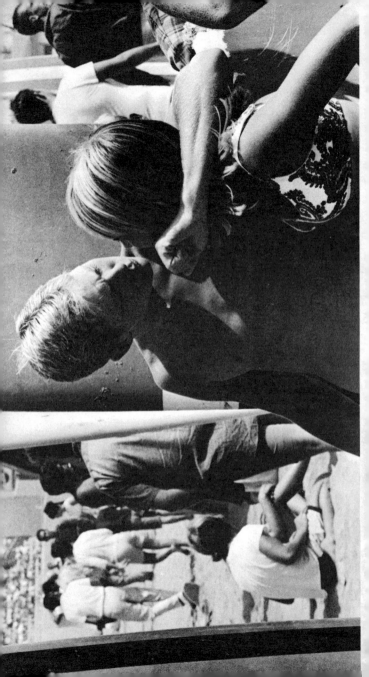

Strong Arm—Claes Oldenburg

"Lazy idle little loafer!" cried the prefect of studies. "Break my glasses! An old schoolboy trick. Out with your hand."

Stephen closed his eyes and held out in the air his trembling hand with the palm upwards. He felt the prefect touch it for a moment at the fingers to straighten it and then the swish of the sleeve of the soutane as the pandybat was lifted to strike. A hot burning stinging tingling blow like the loud crack of a broken stick made his trembling hand crumple together like a leaf in the fire: and at the sound and the pain scalding tears were driven into his eyes. His whole body was shaking with fright, his arm was shaking and his crumpled burning livid hand shook like a loose leaf in the air. A cry sprang to his lips, a prayer to be let off. But though the tears scalded his eyes and his limbs quivered with pain and fright he held back the hot tears and the cry that scalded his throat.

"Other hand!" shouted the prefect of studies.

Stephen drew back his maimed and quivering right arm and held out his left hand. The soutane sleeve swished again as the pandybat was lifted and a loud crashing sound and a fierce maddening tingling burning pain made his hand shrink together with the palms and fingers in a livid quivering mass. The scalding water burst forth from his eyes and, burning with shame and agony and fear, he drew back his shaking arm in terror and burst out into a whine of pain. His body shook with a palsy of fright and in shame and rage he felt the scalding cry come from his throat and the scalding tears falling out of his eyes and down his flaming cheeks.

"Kneel down!" cried the prefect of studies.

. . . And as he knelt . . . he thought of the hand which he had held out in the air with the palms up and of the firm touch of the prefect when he had steadied the shaking fingers and of the beaten swollen reddened mass of palm and fingers that shook helplessly in the air.—James Joyce, *A Portrait of the Artist as a Young Man*

Subtle
Images

Many people are on guard in this competitive world: they want privacy; they are afraid of happenings; or they cannot express their own ideas or feelings. For them, the best defense is a cool face.

Therefore, the discovery of character is often based on the subtlest, the most momentary evidence. A revealing gesture or expression may come and go so fast that an inexperienced observer misses it entirely, or sees it fuzzily.

In the following images the artist has focused on small but telltale signs, so that you have time to discover the meaning of relationships, since a series of tiny details may unite to express a large and important element of character.

Or it may be that an impression of character is created by the spirit of the whole image. You may not be able to identify this quality by referring to visible details, but you may, with your sixth sense, convey the impression by the force of language. Without question, the interpretation of character is in part a personal reaction, and with this section you will move into more intimate and controversial judgments. Since the evidence in these images is less easy to pinpoint, your language will become more and more important. The force and color of words is vital in saying what can't be proved by aiming a finger.

On the opposite page is a bust of an unknown Roman citizen, dating from about 1700 years ago. It is a subtle characterization, without such startling details as the images in the previous section. Try writing a study of the man, based partly on such little things as you can see, and partly on your hunches as to what kind of man he might have been.

It has been suggested you do this on your own, but if you really can't get started, read the characterization on the following page, and the analysis of how it works.

MACARIO

The following characterization of the gentleman on the previous page was written after careful study of the bust itself in its Italian museum.

> The face is that of an unknown man of the third century A. D. Looking at it one has no doubt that it is a speaking likeness, the whimsical expression, the sidelong glance and humorous mouth are so vividly portrayed and the whole is so infused with life that it seems this is someone we know and not an anonymous man who died 1700 years ago . . . one is tempted to think that he was the typical man in the street or Forum in Rome of the decadence, who whiled away his time among pleasant company in the baths and theatre. . . . This anonymous man represents the disillusionment of his own epoch. This amiable cynicism does not conceal the alert intelligence which makes such a vivid impression, and we have the uneasy feeling that perhaps his shade stands mockingly watching us.—Georgina Masson, *The Companion Guide to Rome*

Miss Masson's understanding of quiet detail is revealed in the accuracy of "sidelong glance," and the suggestiveness of "humorous mouth." What she means by "humorous" is probably the slight beginning curl of a smile which lifts the mustache, ever so slightly. This hint of motion combines with the thinking, twinkling eyes to justify the phrases "vividly portrayed" and "infused with life."

It is less easy to say that the generalizations "amiable cynicism" and "alert intelligence" are based on any visible details; they are more accurately described as the result of a sixth-sense impression of the spirit of the whole image. The force and color of language is illustrated in strong words like "disillusionment," "decadence," and "mockingly." A less imaginative observer would have probably said "feeling" for "disillusionment."

Arriving at the Beach—Angostino Raff

Untitled Plexiglass and Wood, 1965—Robert Graham

Woman with an Ermine–Leonardo da Vinci

Don Ramón—Goya

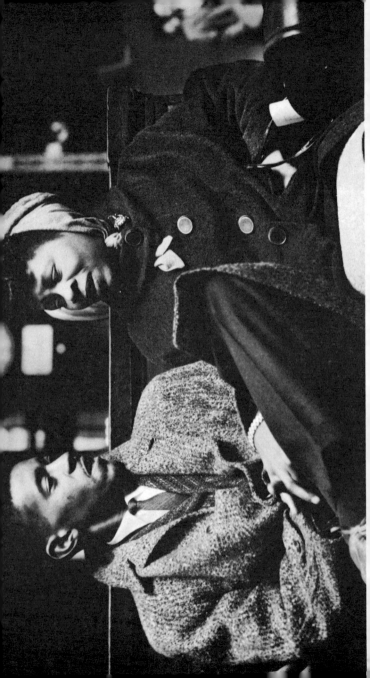

Costume, Background & Props

Among the elements that distinguish a good photograph from the ordinary snapshot are costume, background, and props. In the former the artist chooses a good subject, and then moves to a good position where everything his camera records will add to the characterization. Other people just push the button and hope for a good picture.

Traditional artists have a great advantage over photographers because they can emphasize character by rigid control over what appears behind and around and on the main figure. There is no danger of a truck or a pedestrian moving across the easel to distract from the major point. Painters, sculptors, cartoonists and writers can put in just what they want, and leave out everything else.

In the following images, one primary assignment is to decide on the nature of the main figure, and then describe what the environment contributes. Does anything—line, shape, object, dress, or another person—repeat the qualities of the subject? Pay particular attention to the quality of things, both in themselves and in relation to people, especially their possessors. Compare the homemade guitar on page 64 with the microphone across the page. Also, compare the manner of holding these instruments. Write a brief explanation of how the players and their instruments complement each other to produce a unified characterization.

In some of the other images, show that the environment, by being different from the main figure, heightens a person's character by contrast. Can you find an extreme example of this contrast: a picture where the background is more powerful than the characters? Is there any image where condemnation or laughter is suggested by anything the artist has put next to his subject?

You might also consider whether in any one image the costume, the background, or props reflect personality rather than character.

James Stuart—Anthony Van Dyck

Handball—Ben Shahn

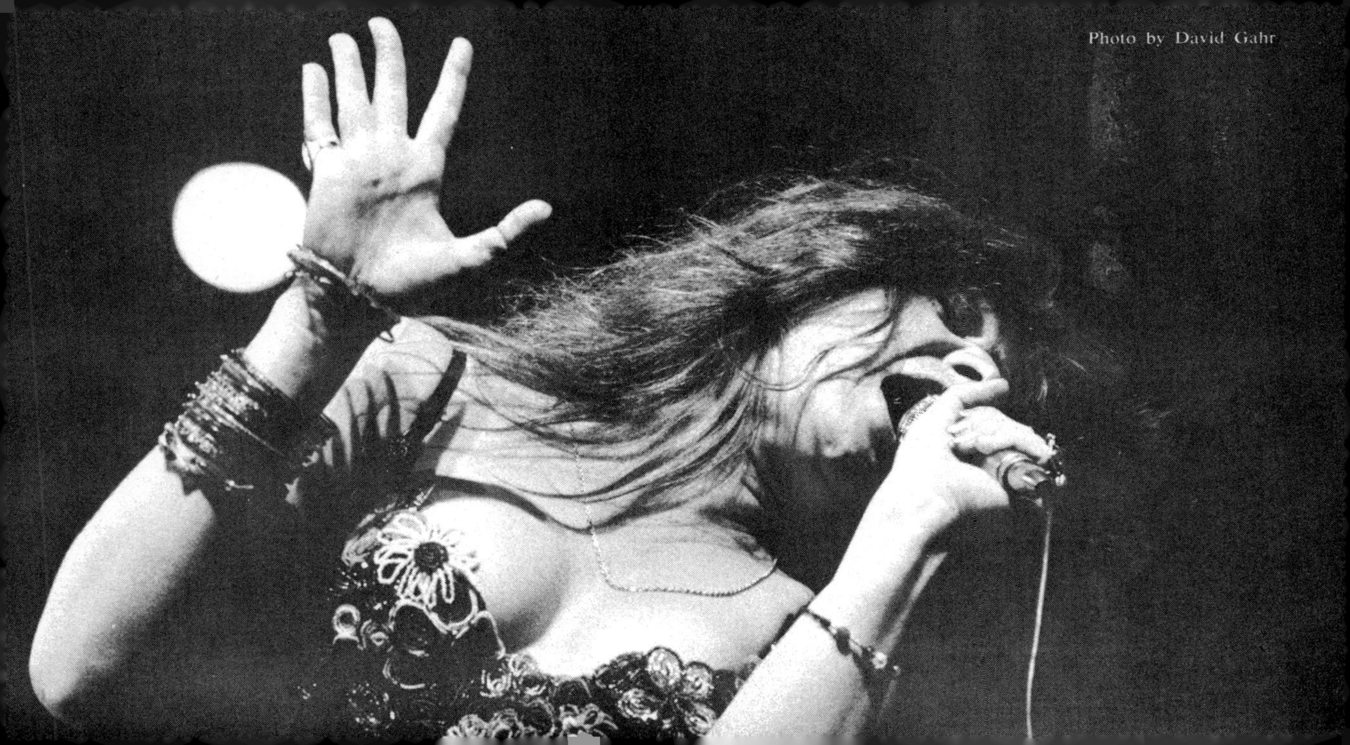
Photo by David Gahr

Colonel Cathcart was a very large, pouting, broad-shouldered man with close-cropped curly dark hair that was graying at the tips and an ornate cigarette holder that he purchased the day before he arrived in Pianosa to take command of his group. He displayed the cigarette holder grandly on every occasion and had learned to manipulate it adroitly. Unwittingly, he had discovered deep within himself a fertile aptitude for smoking with a cigarette holder. As far as he could tell, his was the only cigarette holder in the whole Mediterranean theater of operations, and the thought was both flattering and disquieting. He had no doubts at all that someone as debonair and intellectual as General Peckem approved of his smoking with a cigarette holder, even though the two were in each other's presence rather seldom, which in a way was very lucky, Colonel Cathcart recognized with relief, since General Peckem might not have approved of his cigarette holder at all. When such misgivings assailed Colonel Cathcart, he choked back a sob and wanted to throw the damned thing away, but he was restrained by his unswerving conviction that the cigarette holder never failed to embellish his masculine, martial physique with a high gloss of sophisticated heroism that illuminated him to dazzling advantage among all the other full colonels in the American Army with whom he was in competition.—Joseph Heller, *Catch-22*

New York Movie–Edward Hopper

Lady Dalkeith—John Merton

Primavera (detail)—Sandro Botticelli

Roman graffiti

Human Relationships

A Few People

What is the essential relationship between the two or three people represented on the next nine pages? Where are they? Who are they? Why are they there? What do you imagine they are thinking and saying?

What is the basis of the relationship: agreement, sympathy, and affection; or distance, tension and conflict? Or is it something else—bewilderment, perhaps—or lack of communication?

Could you write a page of dialogue suggesting the chief aspect of the relationship? Can you imagine the tone of voice of each individual, and find words to fit this personal quality? Remember the point about the temper of emotion made in the Introduction: good dialogue always expresses emotion.

Describe, as though you were writing stage directions, the gestures and expressions revealed in these images. Put your emphasis on showing how the characters feel about each other, and how they are reacting toward each other. If you think conflict is present, either openly or secretly, explain its nature, how intensely it appears to be felt, and what its motives may be.

The more you observe such human relationships and the more you analyze them, the more you will be preparing the kind of material which eventually will go into writing short stories or scenarios for TV and film. Human connections are the absolute foundation for such creative activity.

Finally, a more difficult assignment for this chapter is to imagine that one individual is quite self-conscious about what he is doing: he has a particular emotional or intellectual attitude toward his own actions. Write a stream-of-consciousness piece expressing this relationship. Or, write a brief characterization based on the connection between thought and action. This assignment is a useful exercise in exposition, whether in writing nonfiction or fiction. In most of the world's great novels, for example, there is conflict within the main character, between what he thinks and what he feels, as against what he actually does.

Trio-Walt Kuhn

The Two Friends—Ernst Kirchner

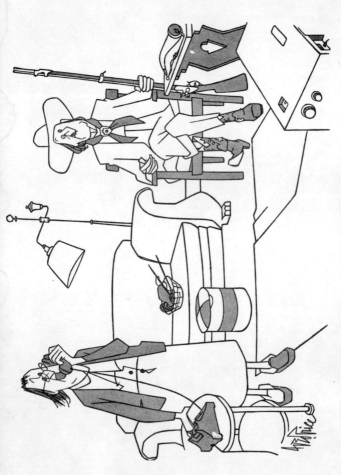

"We're not watching any show.
I'm afraid we've watched one too many already."

Canasta—Mario Cimara

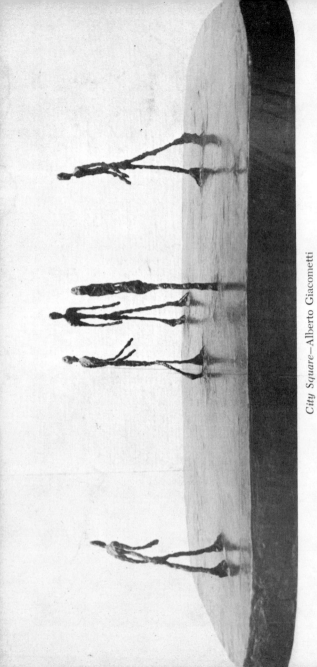

City Square—Alberto Giacometti

The car turned in at the brief, crescent-shaped drive and waited until the two cabs ahead had pulled away. The car pulled up, the doorman opened the rear door, a little man got out. The little man nodded pleasantly enough to the doorman and said "Wait" to the chauffeur. "Will the Under Secretary be here long?" asked the doorman.

"Why?" said the little man.

"Because if you were going to be here, sir, only a short while, I'd let your man leave the car here, at the head of the rank."

"Leave it there ANYWAY," said the Under Secretary.

"Very good, sir," said the doorman. He saluted and frowned only a little as he watched the Under Secretary enter the hotel.

"Well," said the doorman to himself, "it was a long time coming. It took him longer than most, but sooner or later all of them. . . ."

He opened the door of the next car, addressed a colonel and a major by their titles, and never did anything about the Under Secretary's car, which pulled ahead and parked in the drive.—John O'Hara, opening paragraphs of short story, "Graven Image."

In this brief image of a relationship, the attitude of each man toward the other is suggested by dialogue.

What led the "little man" to say, "Leave it there ANYWAY"? In what tone of voice did he say it?

The attitude of the doorman toward the "little man," and toward the situation in general, is suggested by his salute and then his little frown.

Then the full nature of their relationship is indicated by what the doorman says to himself, and what he does about the little man's car.

Write a brief analysis explaining all the conflicting ideas and emotions, especially those that the author does not set down in words. Keep in mind that everything that happens between the two men is the direct result of their relationship, which clearly has existed for some time.

Large Groups
of People

There is so much more to see here—so many more individual characters and so many human relationships that you should find material for longer compositions.

As in the previous section, it is important to observe what and who the people are and how they are connected. Also, notice the relations between various groups within the large group. Then try to sense the power of the atmosphere of a crowd. This may be considered as a "character," in that its force may arouse emotion or cause action.

What happens to individual character when it is assaulted or influenced by a group, or a mob? Is there any evidence in these images that some people are playing a role, just because others around them are doing so? If so, it will be important in your characterization. Look back to the journalist's portrait of Robert Kennedy on page 36.

The feeling of a whole scene can be understood from provable details, but also from intuition. To write effectively about atmosphere, you have to use your eyes AND your sixth sense. It may help, after studying the images, to close your eyes and remember. This is important in crowd-watching because details are often smudged by distance. Try judging the character of the scene by fluent elements, such as form, shape, and pattern. What is suggested, for example, by the tipped position of the people in "The Conference" on page 86?

Also, look for variations in the pattern. Is anybody in the crowd "out of it"? Is anybody merely watching as an observer, perhaps a satirical one?

The subject matter of these images will let you practice one of the most important elements in writing: selectivity; the emphasis on one of many ideas, or facts, or characters, and then the appropropriate use and ordering of others so that they contribute to your dominant choice.

American and Russian soldiers after defeat of Nazis

The Last Supper—G. Bassano

The Conference—Peppe Romano

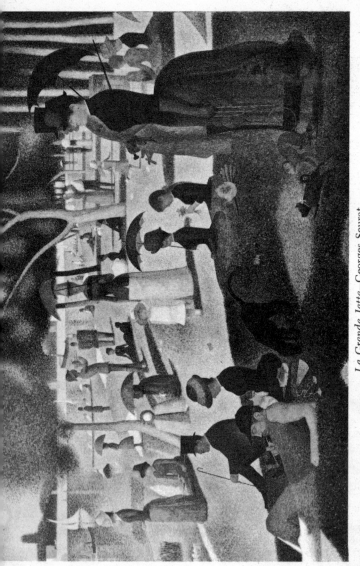

La Grande Jatte—Georges Seurat

Public Relations—Jorge de la Vega

Discothèque 1—Fred S. Hausman

By seven o'clock the orchestra has arrived, no thin five-piece affair, but a whole pitful of oboes and trombones and saxophones and viols and cornets and piccolos, and low and high drums. The last swimmers have come in from the beach now and are dressing upstairs; the cars from New York are parked five deep in the drive, and already the halls and salons and verandas are gaudy with primary colors, and hair bobbed in strange new ways, and shawls beyond the dreams of Castile. The bar is in full swing, and floating rounds of cocktails permeate the garden outside, until the air is alive with chatter and laughter, and casual innuendo and introductions forgotten on the spot, and enthusiastic meetings between women who never knew each other's names.

The lights grow brighter as the earth lurches away from the sun, and now the orchestra is playing yellow cocktail music, and the opera of voices pitches a key higher. Laughter is easier minute by minute, spilled with prodigality, tipped out at a cheerful word. The groups change more swiftly, swell with new arrivals, dissolve and form in the same breath; already there are wanderers, confident girls who weave here and there among the stouter and more stable, become for a sharp, joyous moment the center of a group, and then, excited with triumph, glide on through the sea-change of faces and voices and color under the constantly changing light.

Suddenly one of these gypsies, in trembling opal, seizes a cocktail out of the air, dumps it down for courage and, moving her hands like Frisco, dances out alone on the canvas platform. A momentary hush; the orchestra leader varies his rhythm obligingly for her, and there is a burst of chatter as the erroneous news goes around that she is Gilda Gray's understudy from the *Follies*. The party has begun.—F. Scott Fitzgerald, *The Great Gatsby*

Contradictions in One Image

This chapter poses a new problem: finding how one aspect of character opposes another.

This may mean that some object associated with the character contradicts his expression, or that a gesture or pose does not fit a quality suggested elsewhere in the image. Most important, you may feel that something in the picture suggests inner personal conflict.

Such tensions will be the basis of all assignments in this chapter. Focus on one character, searching for physical details and ideas and feelings that do not fit agreeably with others. The contradiction may be immediately apparent—as when a man wears long hair in curls—or it may be more secret—as in the sculpture pictured on page 99. If you don't understand it, look up the word "paradox."

Think of all the associations that come automatically to mind at sight of the title, the subject matter, the clothing and props, the obvious facial expression. Then look for details, shapes, variations in expression, or an intangible "something" which contradicts those often trite quick judgments. Explain the opposition in expository fashion, or write a monologue by the individual character, revealing the tension. Or you might try creating another character who is watching the person pictured: who is he and what does he see?

This process may lead you to decide that some of these people are not what they appear. If so, you have recognized a very important element in understanding character: the oppositions and contradictions in almost everybody. These are vital to the study of motives, since the essence of an act may be in conflict with its apparent reason. Try describing one of these people in relation to what you imagine might be causing him to look as he does.

Art and Life have one thing in common: they are both rooted in contrast. Every work of art of any value reveals or suggests this fact, and one measure of greatness in art is the depth of its tension. Explain how the forcefulness of one of these images is the result of conflict.

Woman with Cigarette—Guy Pene du Bois

HAMLET [*to his old friends* ROSENCRANTZ *and* GUILDERN-STERN] . . . I have of late—but wherefore I know not—lost all my mirth, forgone all custom of exercises; and, indeed, it goes so heavily with my disposition that this goodly frame, the earth, seems to me a sterile promontory; this most excellent canopy, the air, look you, this brave o'erhanging firmament, this majestical roof fretted with golden fire—why, it appears no other thing to me but a foul and pestilent congregation of vapours. What a piece of work is man! how noble in reason! how infinite in faculty! in form and moving how express and admirable! in action how like an angel! in apprehension how like a god! the beauty of the world! the paragon of animals! And yet, to me, what is this quintessence of dust? Man delights not me; no, nor woman neither . . .
—William Shakespeare, *Hamlet*, Act II, Scene 2

Cardinal Scipione Borghese—Bernini

The Failure—Pietro Annigoni

Woman with a Compass—Caravaggio

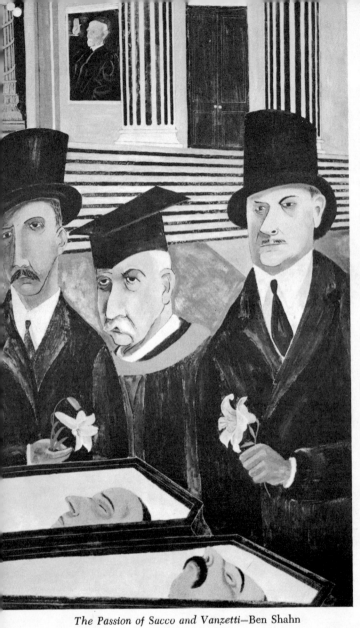

The Passion of Sacco and Vanzetti—Ben Shahn

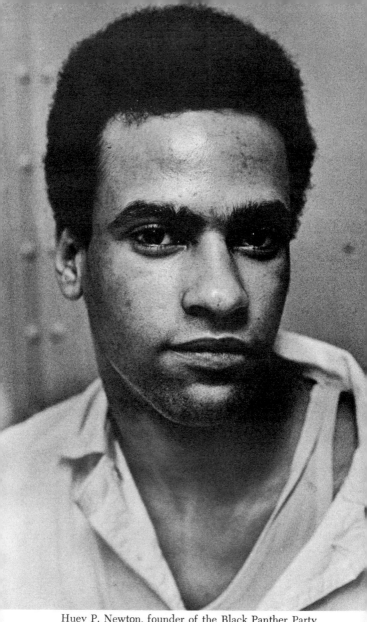

Huey P. Newton, founder of the Black Panther Party

Here are two different ways of writing about the contradiction in the photograph on page 97:

A photo of a model in the nude normally suggests
certain provocative ideas, but this picture is different. It would never be printed in cheesecake
magazines. Most cheap photography reveals nudes
who are exploiting their condition for commercial
purposes; if you look at their eyes carefully, you
know they are cynically amused by their naked-
ness.
This girl's eyes contradict her nudity: they are un-
happy, and uninterested. Her hair is long and
stringy, like the lank mother in one of Charles
Addams' cartoons. Her hands, too, are held in a
thoroughly unsexy gesture, as if the studio were
cold. Almost everything about her suggests that
the photographer, faced with an attractive model,
decided to make fun of her natural endowments.

MODEL. What are these shots for?
PHOTOG. Nothing special.
MODEL. Then why in the nude?
PHOTOG. They aren't nude photographs.
MODEL. Then why do I have to pose this way?
PHOTOG. You aren't going to pose at all.
MODEL. That's what I get paid for—posing. What
do you want, anyway?
PHOTOG. I want you to stop talking—stand over
there in the flat light and let your hair
down.
MODEL. Oh, I get it.
PHOTOG. Do you? Arrange your hair down in front
to cover up, partly.
MODEL. Why?
PHOTOG. Because that's the way I want to take the
picture.
MODEL. But what's it supposed to mean?
PHOTOG. We'll see what it looks like.

Changes
of
Time

In this chapter you run into another controversy about character: the meaning of change. Here you will see evidence of what people have been at different times and at different stages of development, and then what they have become.

In some cases, the faces of change are obvious; it will, however, require study and care in writing to describe the alterations accurately and sensitively.

The first problem is the meaning of change: is it for better, or worse? . . . Does the character appear less powerful or stronger? . . . less selfish, or more preoccupied? . . . less controlled, or more serene? . . . undeveloped or more interesting and complicated? . . . more civilized or less? Or should you just say there is a difference? Are there other comparisons, based on your knowledge of people, or what you have read, or what you have seen so far in this book?

Examine the images for differences in expression, in costume, and in suggestions of thought and feeling. Consider whether the images give clues about changes in the character's attitude toward himself. This may be most important in making your judgments.

In some cases, look for external change not matched by some change in character. The kind of contradiction studied in the previous chapter may be relevant here.

If you know other images of the same people, refer to them as evidence of other changes. Assume your reader hasn't seen your own example, and describe precisely the details you remember. There are many other pictures of Lincoln, and of course thousands of photographs of Sophia Loren. Furthermore, it might add to the development of your writing to compare these images with what has often been said and written about such famous people.

There may be a great temptation to hand out cliches: "How old he looks." . . . "You can tell she has been through a lot," etc. . . . etc. . . . etc. These are useless. Write out detailed evidence to show WHY you say what you do.

Or try something entirely different: write a dialogue between the two altered, but same people.

I went back to the Devon School not long ago, and found it looking oddly newer than when I was a student there fifteen years before. It seemed more sedate than I remembered it, more perpendicular and strait-laced, with narrower windows and shinier woodwork, as though a coat of varnish had been put over everything for better preservation. But, of course, fifteen years before there had been a war going on. Perhaps the school wasn't as well kept up in those days; perhaps varnish, along with everything else, had gone to war.

I didn't entirely like this glossy new surface, because it made the school look like a museum, and that's exactly what it was to me, and what I did not want it to be. In the deep, tacit way in which feeling becomes stronger than thought, I had always felt that the Devon School came into existence the day I entered it, was vibrantly real while I was a student there, and then blinked out like a candle the day I left.

Now here it was after all, preserved by some considerate hand with varnish and wax. Preserved along with it, like stale air in an unopened room, was the well-known fear which had surrounded and filled those days, so much of it that I hadn't even known it was there. Because, unfamiliar with the absence of fear and what that was like, I had not been able to identify its presence.

Looking back now across fifteen years, I could see with great clarity the fear I had lived in, which must mean that in the interval I had succeeded in a very important undertaking: I must have made my escape from it.—
John Knowles, *A Separate Peace*

Lincoln in 1860

Lincoln in 1863

Sophia Loren as a young actress

Sophia Loren at the height of her career

The Photographer then

The Photographer now

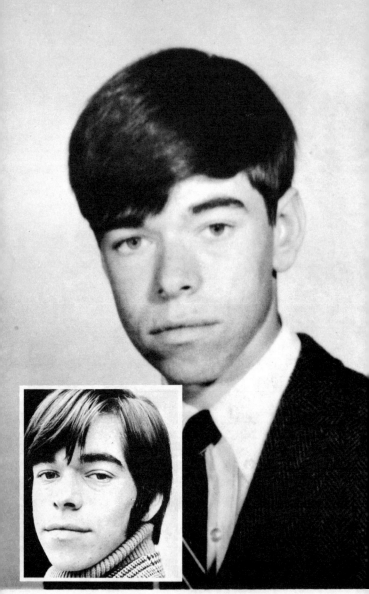

10th grade Inset, 12th grade

Blow-up

The device of this chapter can be used anywhere.

Suppose you see a small group arguing. They are some distance away, so you cannot make out details. Your first impression is simple and emotional: the conflict is noisy and irritated.

As you move in closer, the obvious sights may begin to change, turning into something more complex than you first thought. The general tone of anger may be divided into different degrees of temper. Conflicts and contrasts may appear among those on the same side. Various roles may develop: a real battler, a detached observer, a frightened one.

The closer you get, the more difficult it becomes to unify your own view of the whole situation. You try to study one, then another, then another personality; eventually, you settle on one interesting or dramatic individual, or small group. In this process of cutting and choosing, you are like a photographer making a blow-up, as you will see in the pictures that follow.

Observe the character of specific people as they grow larger and larger; try to understand their relationships to each other, which were uncertain at a distance. Consider your own feelings too: do they change as the scene grows smaller and smaller?

At the end go back and compare the large, whole scene with the pin points, and decide whether one complements the other and clarifies it, or whether by competing visually and emotionally, they leave you with an ambiguous impression of the character of the scene.

Write an imaginative re-creation of the scene from your point of view, as if you were in the middle of it. Then describe the same scene from a distance.

On the opposite page is an example of a professional novelist's use of the blow-up device. It is a brief moment in a story about two white ivory traders trying to cope with conditions in the jungles of Africa. Write a similar passage, beginning with general, abstract ideas, and ending with a tiny detail of character.

The two white traders lived like blind men in a large room, aware only of what came in contact with them (and of that only imperfectly), but unable to see the general aspect of things. The river, the forest, all the great land throbbing with life, were like a great emptiness. Even the brilliant sunshine disclosed nothing intelligible. Things appeared and disappeared before their eyes in an unconnected and aimless kind of way. The river seemed to come from nowhere and flow nowhither. It flowed through a void. Out of that void, at times, came canoes and men with spears in their hands would suddenly crowd the yard of the station. They were naked, glossy black, ornamented with snowy shells and glistening brass wire, perfect of limb. They made an uncouth babbling noise when they spoke, moved in a stately manner, and sent quick, wild glances out of their startled, never-resting eyes.

Those warriors would squat in long rows, four or more deep, before the veranda, while their chiefs bargained for hours over an elephant tusk. Kayerts, the short fat trader, sat on his chair and looked down on the proceedings, understanding nothing. He stared at them with his round blue eyes, called out to Carlier: "Here, look! look at that fellow there—and that other one, to the left. Did you ever see such a face? Oh, the funny brute!"

Carlier, the thin trader, smoking native tobacco in a short wooden pipe, swaggered up twirling his mustaches, and surveyed the warriors with haughty indulgence.—Joseph Conrad, "An Outpost of Progress"

A Matter of Interpretation

The Graphic
Arts

Students would be surprised to read the contradictory reports handed in by teachers and advisors:

> This boy is insolent. He's a lazy type. He is too big for his britches and ought to be cut down to size.
> He works very slowly and painfully and gets very angry at himself. Sometimes this makes him look sour and cocky. He isn't; he's just thoroughly uncertain.

These characterizations of the same student are very much like the interpretations which different artists make of the same person. The variations are so startling that the observer may wonder if the subjects ARE the same.

Since they are, you should consider the following questions, as you study the contradictions: Are you looking at two completely different sides of the same person? Or one realistic and one more abstract portrait? Or one deliberately critical and one nicely favorable vision? Or one sloppy interpretation by a bad artist and one of genuine understanding by a man of great perception? Or one view of a quirk of personality and another of a profound truth of human nature?

Your answers may suggest that different concepts of the same individual reveal more about the artist than his subject. Look carefully at the selection of props, costume and background, as in the photographs of Ernest Hemingway. Look at the specific act and expression which the artist chose to present.

For each juxtaposed pair write an explanation of essential differences, emphasizing whether these are the result of contrasts in the artists' purposes, peculiarities of the diverse media, or differences in what the subject allowed to appear.

Two of the images interpret two "types" from two different social periods—the drawing on page 134 and the painting that follows it. Are the two "characters" alike? Are the artists' personal attitudes the same?

Statue of Saint Francis

Head of Christ—Georges Roualt

Christ Cutting Down the Cross—Jose Clemente Orozco

Ernest Hemingway

Ernest Hemingway

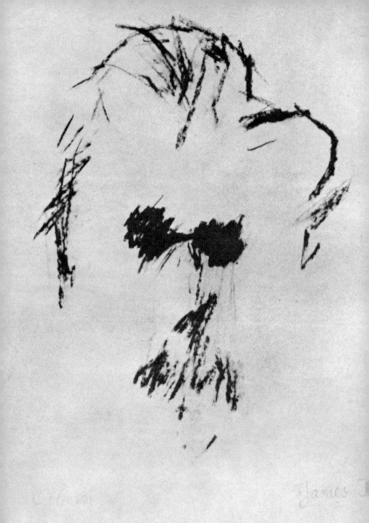

James Thurber—Robert Osborn

James Thurber

Girl—John Held, Jr.

Beat Girl—Emmanuele Pandolfini

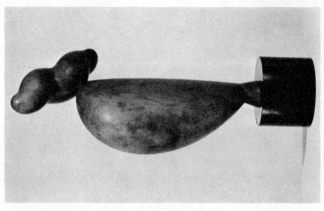

Nancy Cunard–Constantin Brancusi

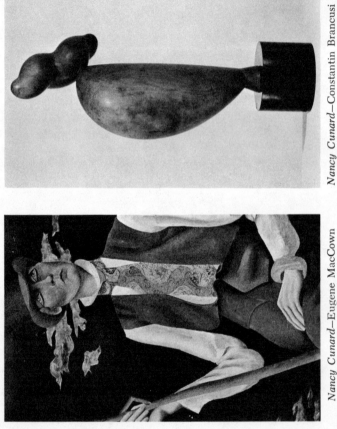

Nancy Cunard–Eugene MacCown

136

Characterization
in Acting

Since abstract generalizing in composition is often superficial, trite, and unconvincing, young writers should study a technique of characterization which is just the opposite: good acting. An effective performer is thorough, sensuous, and persuasive.

The pictures that follow reveal many devices used in the theater, TV, the cinema, to portray and suggest character. Observe these images carefully, and then translate the visual effects into words.

Two special aspects of these pictures should be mentioned. In some cases, the situation and the emotions are well known, are obvious, or are explained. In others you will have to guess what is happening and who the characters are. What you write in either case depends on how you believe the physical details of performance are related to the intangibles of emotions, traits, and motives.

Where you know what is going on, as in *Othello,* ask yourself if the actors reveal anything new about the character of the "characters." Where you don't know, as in the new play photographed on page 146, explain why you think the physical evidence suggests a certain happening and certain attitudes and emotions.

Finally, there is the question of genuine characterization. As you watch a performance, or study an image, are you more conscious of the name and fame of the actor, or of the essential traits of a created character? You will know you are watching a true characterization when you find yourself thinking of the character's name rather than that of the actor's—Richard Burton, say—and when the performer's visage, gestures, and voice suggest someone who exists only in imagination, like Mrs. Robinson in the film *The Graduate.*

Harold Lloyd in *The Freshman*

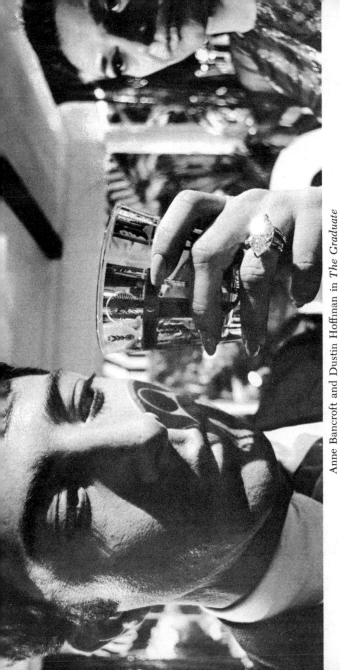

Anne Bancroft and Dustin Hoffman in *The Graduate*

Laurence Olivier and Frank Finley in *Othello*

Orson Welles and Dorothy Comingore in *Citizen Kane*

Martita Hunt and John Carradine in
The Madwoman of Chaillot

THE RAGPICKER. Countess, little by little, the pimps
have taken over the world. They don't do anything,
they don't make anything—they just stand there
and take their cut. I remember well the time when
a cabbage could sell itself just by being a cabbage.
Nowadays it's no good being a cabbage—unless
you have an agent and pay him a commission.
These days, Countess, every cabbage has its pimp.
—Jean Giraudoux, *The Madwoman of Chaillot*

142

Student actors after the murder of Julius Caesar

Bonnie and Clyde in real life

Faye Dunaway and Warren Beatty in *Bonnie and Clyde*

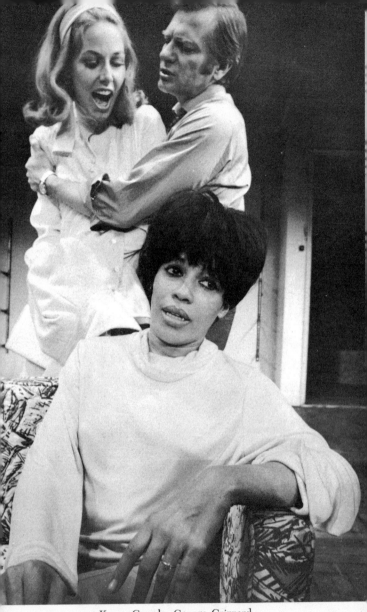

Karen Grassle, George Grizzard,
Diana Sands in *The Gingham Dog*

Non-
realistic
Images

In the previous chapter, truth about character was suggested through imitation; here, it lies in distortion and fancy.

The point in these images is not whether the concrete art gives a recognizable picture of human character— as before—but how the strange visual facts communicate man's nature almost in spite of themselves. Do these non-realistic shapes create for you the peculiar atmosphere of certain feelings or traits? Do they by their grotesque combinations, reveal new impulses in other people?

One approach here is to focus on the essential distortion. Is its grossness, or fancy, or chaos, related to some gross, fanciful, or chaotic elements in man's character? Is there something significant about the peculiar sizes, forms, and connections in the symbols of men and women on the next pages? Is the position of evil in Klee's picture important?

Sometimes the virtue of strange and curious pictures is that they suddenly clarify for you hints and guesses which you have felt but never quite understood. This can be particularly true of analogies, and you might try explaining how one of these images made you see what certain people are really like.

Before you write, study all the images, and then the opening paragraphs of a surrealistic short story, "The Door," by E. B. White, on page 153. The commentary on page 152 may show you how to use this passage in relation to your own writing.

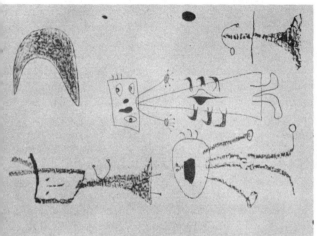

Women—Joan Miró

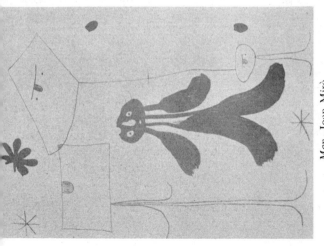

Men—Joan Miró

Helmet Head No. 1—Henry Moore

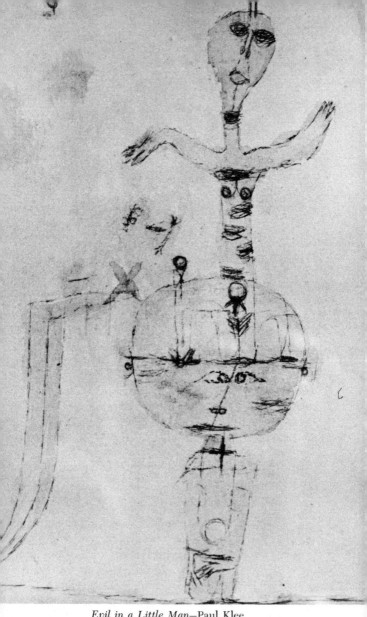

Evil in a Little Man–Paul Klee

In all the images in this chapter the effect on the observer is startling for two main reasons, both of which are important for good writing: the invention of "things" that do not exist, and the combining of strange and bewildering ideas and facts.

Look particularly at the extraordinary clothing created for the female figure on page 155, and then the bizarre relationships revealed on page 156. These two images were chosen especially to emphasize the fact that much poor writing is the result of a particular kind of poor observation and thought: noticing only normal things, and arranging them in perfectly normal connections.

In the passage on the opposite page, you will see how one writer achieved the effect of originality by inventing new details, and then forcing things together in unusual combinations. Look at the names he created— "duroid" and "flexsan"—and the collision of images in "a washable house."

Try inventing a creature of your own; or imagine a grotesque or fanciful combination of objects and people. Try making up a bizarre individual and then putting him in a commonplace situation; or do the opposite, by introducing ordinary people into wild places. In one of his greatest stories, H. G. Wells sent his main character into a ferocious storm in the mountains, and when he came out, he was in a country where everybody was blind. The results create extraordinary effects of characterization.

In dealing with non-realistic images, you have a clear choice: either expressing direct relationships with realistic existence, or just giving hints. Before writing a final version, you should be sure which technique you are following.

Everything (he kept saying) is something it isn't. And everybody is always somewhere else. Maybe it was the city, being in the city, that made him feel how queer everything was and that it was something else. Maybe (he kept thinking) it was the names of the things. The names were tex and frequently koid. Or they were flex and oid, or they were duroid (sani) or flexsan (duro), but everything was glass (but not quite glass) and the thing that you touched (the surface, washable, crease-resistant) was rubber, only it wasn't quite rubber and you didn't quite touch it but almost. The wall, which was glass but thrutex, turned out on being approached not to be a wall, it was something else, it was an opening or doorway—and the doorway (through which he saw himself approaching) turned out to be something else, it was a wall. And what he had eaten not having agreed with him.

He was in a washable house, but he wasn't sure. Now about those rats, he kept saying to himself. He meant the rats that the Professor had driven crazy by forcing them to deal with problems which were beyond the scope of rats, the insoluble problems.—E. B. White, Opening lines of short story, "The Door"

The Dream—Max Beckmann

The Walk—Richard Lindner

a copper plate, a zinc plate, a rubber towel, 2 calipers,
1 drainpipe telescope and a roaring man—Max Ernst

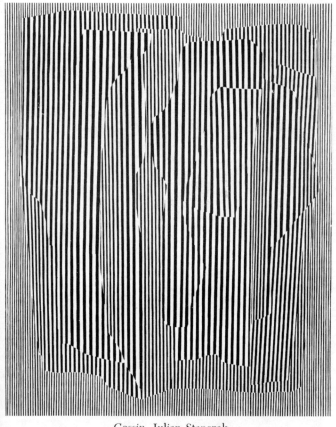

Gossip–Julian Stanczak

The Watchers—Lynn Chadwick

Part II

Part I stressed important techniques of observation and thinking about character, both in art and actual existence. When these techniques are developed and refined—like the search for subtleties, and the evaluation of comparisons—they can be transferred to writing, with profit for writer and reader.

In this second part, new images have been organized into six areas of subject matter, as a basis for testing all the techniques previously presented, To understand and write convincingly about Children, or Emotion, or "Character," for example, you need to be conscious of outstanding details, contradictions, acting and "acting," costume, and the other elements of characterization.

As one specific assignment, go through the images looking for nothing but subtlety of characterization, and write a description of your discoveries. Or, pick images from different sections and relate them to "playing a role."

Most important in Part II is a new emphasis on the writing of short stories. Study all images from the point of view of dialogue and narrative. Observe them from the single most important aspect of character in fiction: internal or external conflict that causes action—*plot*. Imagine what some of these individuals would do in difficult situations, if their desires, say, were frustrated; or imagine what led to the image, or what came after it. Here is where a story may begin.

Who or what is an individual looking at, or speaking to? What may he be thinking or saying, in the circumstances? What might his statements make someone else do? The answers may produce material for plots.

As a classic example, there is the fact that the act of blaming somebody—as reflected in the "Peanuts" cartoon on page 163—has been used by many, many successful story writers throughout the years: Poe's "The Cask of Amontillado," Thurber's "The Secret Life of Walter Mitty," and Hemingway's "My Old Man."

Children

When I was a child, I spake as a child, I understood as a child, I thought as a child! but when I became a man, I put away childish things.

What are the true characteristics of children? Are they childish, cute or insecure? . . . joyful, imaginative, selfish? cruel, undisciplined, curious, and nonintellectual? Or are these just clichés?

Are there any childish traits which really should be put away by adults, for the benefit of individuals and society? One great problem in the modern world is lack of agreement on which is which. In some of these images you may find an answer.

Look for pictures that dramatize those attitudes and feelings which are short-lived responses to a child's peculiar existence, and also those which are eternal qualities of human nature, at all ages.

Socially, how do children differ from adults, or those who are called adults? Begin by questioning some of the most obvious and hackneyed assumptions: Adults are less selfish? . . . less belligerent? . . . less loose? . . . more thoughtful? . . . more mature? (What does that mean?) . . . or more organized? Pick one image in this section and show how it reveals the same—or different —characteristics as some adult pictured in any other section in the book. Imagine the child in the adult situation, and vice versa, and then narrate the results in story form.

Your conclusions depend on reading the expressions, gestures, and other signs, just as you did in Part I. Before you think or write anything, observe the sensuous evidence accurately and imaginatively, both in specific individuals and their connections with others.

Try to imagine what thoughts, feelings, motives—the things not seen—made these children look as they do. That is the right approach to understanding character, whether you are watching it unfold in a story, a novel, a film, or trying to make your own characters act out a story.

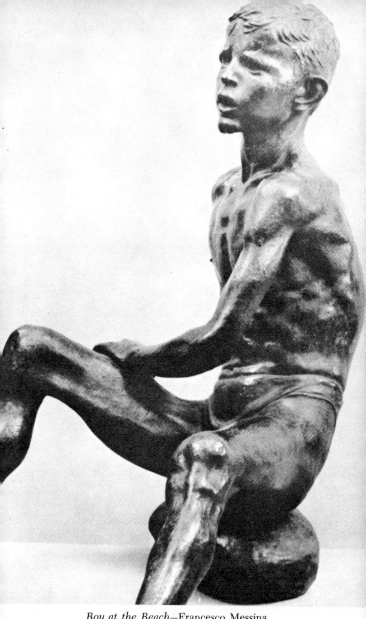

Boy at the Beach—Francesco Messina

Boy with Frogs

Under his relentless eye,
Jarred and jeered,
The small frogs hop
And pulse in their
Suddenly glass world.

He, blond and curious,
Captive and captivated,
Holds in his hands
World of water, pebbles, grass
And the power
Of topsy-turvy and crash.

But he is content
To study them a while,
With their delicate legs
Pressed against the glass,
The futile leaps to freedom
And their frantic eyes.

It's a game for a God
Of course.
Later, the vibrant frogs,
Still leaping with protest
And life, are forgotten
On a shelf. He is out
Wondering about the waterbugs.

                              Sy Kahn

Another Generation

What happens to human attitudes in high school . . . and then in college . . . and then in the first few years of so-called adult life?

Do some girls and boys become more critical, more rebellious, and more confused? Do they see different things, and things differently? Are the conflicts different? What about pressure groups: do they force the individual into one mold, either to left or right?

What do you really believe and feel about adults and other authorities? Really—not just for show?

The images here will present young people in a variety of attitudes and situations. Some are ambiguous, revealing the same traits already presented in children's lives, and those that will come for adults. Some suggest that the lack of a valid name for the now generation is owing to a lack of truly typical characteristics. More and more, for example, it is being recognized that the trite "teen-ager" does nothing but name a physical fact (although it is a handy label for manufacturers and magazines).

Can you find in these pictures truthful evidence of your own feelings and attitudes? Can you put these into words? Or are they wordless? Could you make up actions to suggest your own character, without literally naming the traits?

Can you find evidence of what is false—the "put-on"? Or is that a basic characteristic?

In cases where conflict is suggested, try writing a story leading up to the scene, or following it.

Imagine that a boy, or girl, or adult—or a policeman— or a famous character—walks into the scene. What would people do, or say?

Often a good story can be made out of the difference between what a young person does and his own attitude toward what he does. Does this apply to the Parisian trio on page 172?

Bobby, the famous young athlete, shrugged his shoulders, surveyed the floor, slipped his hand in his pocket to count his change, and finally, got up and went out for a coke. He exchanged sarcastic remarks with a couple of guys, but kept watching Jody. Seeing that her date had not returned, Bobby put down the empty bottle and strolled casually back to the chair next to Jody. He managed to kick an ashtray as he sat down, but as she said nothing, he lapsed back into his previous silence.

Five minutes passed while Bobby stared blandly off into space. Finally, Jody leaned over: "You think quite a bit of yourself, don't you?"

"Oh, I don't know," said Bobby. "If I don't like me who will?"

"That's just what I mean," went on Jody. "You always act so blasé. I watched you at a couple of parties, and you look bored by it all, and would people please leave you alone. You make people feel unwanted when they meet you. People like to feel wanted, you know."

Bobby looked at her for a few moments trying to decide whether to laugh or say something profound. Finally, he said quite seriously, "Did it ever occur to you that people who don't really know me, don't really understand me?"

"I don't believe you understand yourself," said Jody.

"If you want me to, I'll explain myself to you. But I'm afraid I'd fascinate you too much," Bobby muttered.

"If you're going to be that way about it, don't bother," Jody said, slightly peeved, "but if you want to be serious, go ahead."

Bobby looked at her quizzically and then plunged on quickly. "You don't realize how much I hate to go out to parties. I always feel at a great disadvantage with strangers because they seem to expect me to do something clever. You may think that sounds conceited, but I think it is true. Since I have gained some fame, and I do go away to school, people my age always seem a little disappointed that I'm not the life of the party."
—From a student short story

Apparitions—Antero Piletti

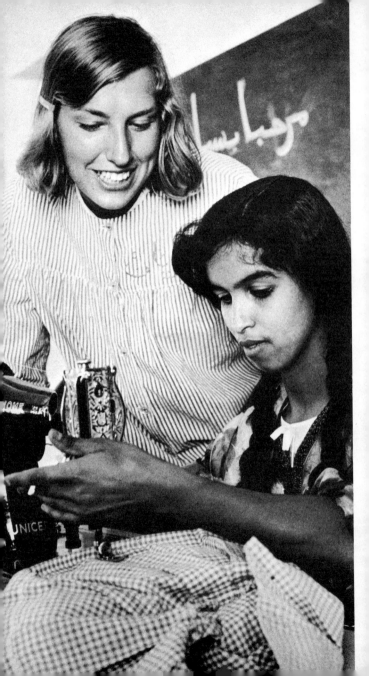

"My goodness, Henry, you're much too young to
be going *har-rumph*, *har-rumph* all the time!"

Between the
Generations

How honest and truthful is one age to another? Are
there times when both are really being themselves so
that one can trust the other? It is so easy and such fun
to play a role for those who are older, or younger,
than you are. Also, sometimes it is necessary to pro-
tect yourself, no matter how old you are, by hiding
behind a puppet personality. When you are with
people of a different age, the character you display—
or the one you put away—depends on what you want,
and what you think others will think of what you
want.

Reactions to what you do will vary from curiosity to
skepticism, to outrage, to embarrassment, and it is
important to decide which is revealed in the following
images. Out of these images it is possible to construct
a series of actions—as is demonstrated in the passage
from Dr. Williams' story on page 189—and thus pre-
pare the foundations for a short story.

Try beginning with the girl's question in the ad on
page 186; then imagine her father's answer, the girl's
next statement, and then a series of cause-and-effect
happenings centering on a conflict between the generations.

Try substituting yourself for one of the people shown.
What would your reactions be in the circumstances?

Write a stream-of-consciousness passage expressing
what some of these individuals may be thinking about
the others who are with them. Write into each person's
thinking concrete evidence of what he has observed.

Write a monologue in which one person tells somebody else what he thinks of what has just been happening. This could lead to another argument, and then
another story.

When you come to Halsmann's portrait at the end of
this section, compare it with his comments on page 21.

An Old Man and His Grandson—Domenico Ghirlandaio

The Music Lesson—Thomas Hart Benton

"But, Daddy, if I don't drink they'll think I'm nowhere."

Now, Dad, what do you say to that?

You could say, and with conviction, that what they think really won't matter. Not if she's sure the way you've taught her is right.

But make no mistake. She's under a lot of pressure from others her own age. Social pressure to be popular—to be one of the crowd. It would be unrealistic to think otherwise.

To stand up to that kind of pressure takes character. And character isn't something a girl is born with. It's something she acquires. Mostly from you, her parents.

If you've taught her well—if you've set a good example, she'll understand that drinking is a pleasure reserved for adults.

She can wait. She has time.

And when that time comes, if she chooses to drink, she'll appreciate drinking for what it is. Something to be enjoyed sensibly. Moderately. Maturely. The way we've always intended the products we sell be enjoyed.

A Father's Day message from... **Seagram** distillers since 1857

For reprints, please write: Advertising Dept., Seagram Distillers Co., 375 Park Ave., N.Y., N.Y. 10022

Going to College—Norman Rockwell

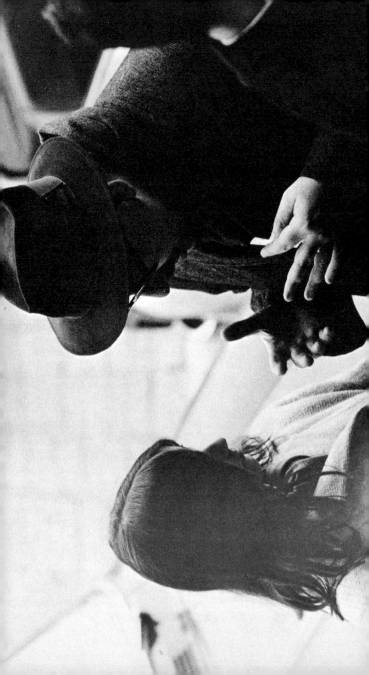

I grasped the child's head with my left hand and tried to get the wooden tongue depressor between her teeth. She fought, with clenched teeth, desperately! But now I also had grown furious—at a child. I tried to hold myself down but I couldn't. I know how to expose a throat for inspection. And I did my best. When finally I got the wooden spatula behind the last teeth and just the point of it into the mouth cavity, she opened up for an instant but before I could see anything she came down again and gripping the wooden blade between her molars she reduced it to splinters before I could get it out again.

Aren't you ashamed, the mother yelled at her. Aren't you ashamed to act like that in front of the doctor?

Get me a smooth-handled spoon of some sort, I told the mother. We're going through with this. The child's mouth was already bleeding. Her tongue was cut and she was screaming in wild hysterical shrieks. Perhaps I should have desisted and come back in an hour or more. No doubt it would have been better. But I have seen at least two children lying in bed dead of neglect in such cases, and feeling that I must get a diagnosis now or never I went at it again. But the worst of it was that I too had got beyond reason. I could have torn the child apart in my own fury and enjoyed it. It was a pleasure to attack her. My face was burning with it.

The damned little brat must be protected against her own idiocy, one says to one's self at such times. Others must be protected against her. It is a social necessity. And all these things are true. But a blind fury, a feeling of adult shame bred of a longing for muscular release are the operatives. One goes on to the end.—William Carlos Williams, "The Use of Force"

"Characters"

They used to be called "characters," and the call echoed a certain wonder, amusement and envy.

Today they are said to be "weirdos," "hippies," and "kooks," and though the wonder may still be there, people with rigid, insecure minds are not amused or envious.

A generation or two ago, it was perfectly all right to have "characters" around, even in the eyes of the Establishment; they were part of the scene. By their eccentric behavior, their clothes, their amusement at the rest of the world, and their lack of interest in rules, they kept everybody else from being too pompous.

Today, when characters appear like those in this section, people with black-and-white minds become annoyed and dictatorial. If young people appear to be "different," parents get upset, counselors are called in, friends take the "victim" aside, and pressure is applied to make them stop being "characters," or perhaps themselves.

These smoke signals dramatize the heart of the problem: the relation between what is and what seems. Two generations ago, an unusual appearance did not mean that a man was evil or dangerous or insane. Today "authorities" seem to think just that. Is it true? What do these images tell you about the difference between what is and what seems? Try inventing a story based on such a conflict.

What does "protest" have to do with the problem? Most of the characters in this section are not necessarily rebellious; they are simply being themselves. They are not trying to force other people to act differently. In other images throughout this book, you will see real protest in action. These call for a different kind of character interpretation, and therefore a different approach in handling a plot.

You could begin by writing a full explanation of the difference between "characters" and "angry young men." Then a story might be created out of a conflict between one of each.

Ancient Roman mosaic

In an arm-chair, with an elbow resting on the table and her head leaning on that hand, sat the strangest lady I have ever seen, or shall ever see.

She was dressed in rich materials—satins, and lace, and silks—all of white. Her shoes were white. And she had a long white veil dependent from her hair, and she had bridal flowers in her hair, but her hair was white. Some bright jewels sparkled on her neck and on her hands, and some other jewels lay sparkling on the table. Dresses, less splendid than the dress she wore, and half-packed trunks, were scattered about. She had not quite finished dressing, for she had but one shoe on—the other was on the table near her hand,—her veil was but half arranged, her watch and chain were not put on, and some lace for her bosom lay with those trinkets, and with her handkerchief, and gloves, and some flowers, and a Prayer-book, all confusedly heaped about the looking-glass.

It was not in the first few moments that I saw all these things, though I saw more of them in the first moments than might be supposed. But, I saw that everything within my view which ought to be white, had been white long ago, and had lost its lustre, and was faded and yellow. I saw that the bride within the bridal dress had withered like the dress, and like the flowers, and had no brightness left but the brightness of her sunken eyes. I saw that the dress had been put upon the rounded figure of a young woman, and that the figure upon which it now hung loose, had shrunk to skin and bone. Once, I had been taken to see some ghastly waxwork at the Fair, representing I know not what impossible personage lying in state. Once, I had been taken to one of our old marsh churches to see a skeleton in the ashes of a rich dress, that had been dug out of a vault under the church pavement. Now, waxwork and skeleton seemed to have dark eyes that moved and looked at me. I should have cried out, if I could.—Charles Dickens, *Great Expectations*

20¢ Movie–Reginald Marsh

The first picture interview in photographic history took place in Paris in 1886. The subject was Marie-Eugene Chevreul, a scientist, on the eve of his 101st birthday. While being photographed, he answered questions about almost everything.

"As for Mr. Charles Darwin, remember that a single error sows the seed of errors! Me, the son of an orangutan . . . NEVER!"

Burlesques and Grotesques

People who use words like "kooks" and "weirdos" should study these next images carefully, for now such language may really be appropriate, along with other words like "burlesques" and "grotesques." In one or two cases you can go further and use "neurotic" and "insane." The spirit and the meanings are different than in the previous section.

This contrast means that in writing about these images, you must write differently. You must imagine differently, too—different scenes, different actions, different conflicts, different solutions. It might be helpful to review the chapter on non-realistic images.

It might also be helpful to consider two specific approaches to short story writing: forcing realistic characters into a fantastic situation, or dropping fantastic characters into a normal, suburban atmosphere. Either will work if done well. For illustration, read several stories by H. G. Wells.

There is another important element in these pictures: the artist's attitude. Is it completely mocking, or is there some sympathy? To use a favorite educational term, what is the artist's "point of view"?

When you have finished a trial piece of writing about these images, you might analyze your own point of view, for here, even more than in the preceding section, you may be faced with your own personality and prejudices. The clues lie in your language.

In fact, this section and the one before it, besides stirring up serious problems in understanding character, also provoke serious problems in language and communication. Probably the language difficulty is more serious than in any other part of the entire book. The reason is that words like "character," "burlesque," "kook," and "neurotic" are often ambiguous as labels of character. What they often do is reveal the character of those who use them. In some cases, they are merely name-calling.

However, don't take all these images seriously: some are just caricatures.

The Mocker Mocked–Paul Klee

The Old Soldier—Leonardo da Vinci

Lewis Payne, who plotted against Lincoln

Faculty Meeting—Hugh Townley

Mother and Son—Carlo Carrà

HARRY. I must have been out of school for only a couple of weeks when . . . it happened. Out of the blue. Disillusionment. Despair. Debilitation. The works. It hit me all at once.

MILT. Oh. Ohhh.

> (HARRY sits on curbstone. MILT puts down white handkerchief, sits beside him.)

HARRY. I remember . . . I was sitting in the park. It was Sunday, a hot, lazy Sunday. The sun was burning on the back of my neck. An open book was on my lap and I was kind of daydreaming, thinking of the future, my plans, my prospects. . . Then suddenly. . . Suddenly I looked up and I saw, standing there in front of me. . . How can I put it in words? It was a dog, Milt. A fox terrier. I'd swear it was a fox terrier. But who knows, I . . .

MILT (interrupting). Let's just say it was a dog, Harry.

HARRY. It was a dog. Right.

MILT. A dog. Go ahead.

HARRY. And. . . And he was there, right in front of me, standing on his hind legs and. . . He looked almost like a little old man with a little white beard and a little wrinkled face. The thing is. . . Milt, he was laughing. He was laughing as loudly and as clearly as I'm talking to you now. I sat there. I couldn't move. I couldn't believe what was happening. And then, he came up to me, now he was walking on all fours and. . . When he got up to me. . . When he got up to me, he raised his leg and . . .

MILT. No.

HARRY (nodding, with twisted expression). All over my gabardine pants. And they were wet through and through. I could swear to that! Then he turned right around and walked off. The whole thing was. . . It was so unreal, all so damn senseless. My mind. . . I thought . . .

> (Emotionally)

Why me? Out of everyone in that park, out of hundreds, thousands of people, why me?—Murray Schisgal, *Luv*

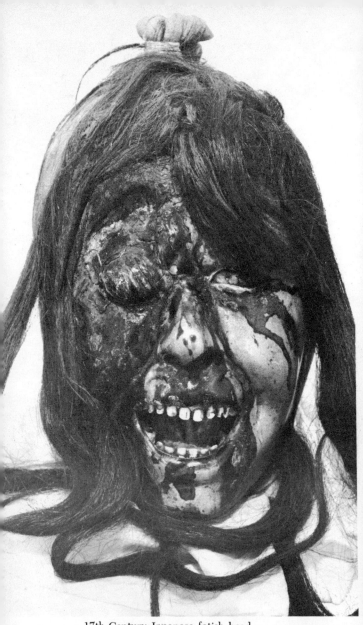

17th-Century Japanese fetish head

Waiting Room—Yannis Gaitis

Illustration for "The Tell-Tale Heart"—Harry Clark

Emotions, Motives, and Storytelling

At the base of all fiction, whether in books, films, or on the stage, there is collision between desire and denial. The more profound and violent the desire, the more dramatic the result when it clashes with denial. Out of this result stream the events of a good story.

One of the great weaknesses of student stories is lack of strong desire in the characters, with the result that very little happens. In fact, hundreds of amateur "stories" have been written which are nothing but tiny scenes, clipped out of life, either before or after something really important happens. In most cases, the characters could at any time in the story just get up and walk out, and it wouldn't make any difference.

As you begin to write fiction, you should probably abandon that favorite student character: the detached observer. He is a trap; get your people into the action.

In this final section, the images have been chosen to focus attention on the temper of strong urgings, their battle with equally strong resistance, and the possibilities of outcome. In most of these, the characters could NOT just get up and go home: the situations involve them too emotionally.

As you study these images, imagine the motives of everybody shown. In some cases you may think they are obvious, as on page 222, and that may make storytelling easier. But then there are others, where you will have to study the display of emotion and guess its reason. If you find a clear answer, you may be able to imagine what such a character would do in another dramatic situation, and there will be the beginnings of a plot.

Finally, in the actual writing, you have a choice: either make the emotion and its motives clear, as in many of Poe's stories—"The Fall of the House of Usher," for instance—or tell the events in such a style as to suggest the motive, as in the tiny tale of Hemingway's on page 221, or Shirley Jackson's "The Lottery."

The Laughers—Renato Guttuso

Woman Weeping—Pablo Picasso

Birthday–Marc Chagall

Marilyn—James F. Gill

Ballad of the Jealous Lover of Lone Green Valley
—Thomas Hart Benton

At two o'clock in the morning two Hungarians got into a cigar store at Fifteenth Street and Grand Avenue. Drevitts and Boyle drove up from the Fifteenth Street police station in a Ford. The Hungarians were backing their wagon out of an alley. Boyle shot one off the seat of the wagon and one out of the wagonbox. Drevitts got frightened when he found they were both dead. "Hell, Jimmy," he said, "you oughtn't to have done it. There's liable to be a hell of a lot of trouble." "They're crooks, aint they?" said Boyle. "They're wops, aint they? Who the hell is going to make any trouble?" "That's all right maybe this time," said Drevitts, "but how did you know they were wops when you bumped them off?"

"Wops," said Boyle, "I can tell wops a mile off." — Ernest Hemingway, "In Our Time"

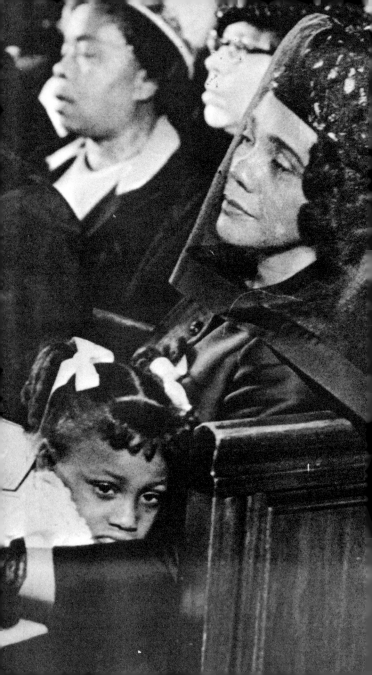

Picture Credits

Picture Credits

Dartmouth College / 130 Karsh / 131 John Bryson / 132 Downtown Gallery / 133 Hans Namuth / 134 Courtesy of Mrs. John Held, Jr. / 136 (top) Professor Hugh Ford / 136 (bottom) John D. Schiff / 138 The Museum of Modern Art / 139 Bob Willoughby, Lee Gross Associates / 140 Roddy McDowall, Lee Gross Associates /141 British Film Institute / 142 Bob Golby Studios / 143 Hart Leavitt / 144 Wide World Photos / 145 Warner Bros-Seven Arts, Inc. / 146 SCOPE Associates / 149 (top) Courtesy Dr. Franco Valli, Rome / 149 (bottom) French Reproduction Rights, Inc. / 150 The Tate Gallery, London / 151 Iolas Galate Gallery, Rome / 154 Courtesy Morton D. May / 155 Courtesy Mildred W. Gosman / 156 Max Ernst, Collection Hans Arp / 157 Martha Jackson Gallery, Inc. / 158 Greater London Council / 161 Gallery of Modern Art, Rome / 162 Hart Leavitt / 163 United Feature Syndicate / 164 Norma Holt /165 Hart Leavitt / 167 R. N. Keith / 168 Hart Leavitt / 170 Anre Karlsson / 171 Bill Eppridge, LIFE Magazine © Time Inc. / 172 Pictorial Parade, Inc. / 174 Galleria Obelisco, Rome / 175 Ruth-Marion Baruch and Perkle Jones / 176 Courtesy Roy Hoopes / 177 Rolf Williams / 178 George Strock, LIFE Magazine © Time Inc. / 179 Stephen G. Perrin / 180 Donald Reilly; Copyright © 1967 THE NEW YORKER Magazine, Inc. / 182 Courtesy Julian Levy / 183 Louvre, Paris / 184 Hart Leavitt / 185 Associated American Artists / 186 Seagram Distillers Company / 187 Curtis Publishing Company / 188 Christopher D. Kirkland / 190 Philippe Halsman / 192 Bill Eppridge, LIFE Magazine © Time Inc. / 193 Institution of Civil Engineers / 194 Agenzia Olympia di Milano / 195 Hart Leavitt / 196 Gordon A. Stevens / 198 John Benton Harris / 199 Whitney Museum of American Art / 200 George Eastman House / 202 The Museum of Modern Art. Gift of J. B. Newmann / 203 British Museum / 204 Library of Congress / 205 Addison Gallery of American Art / Dr. Emilio Jesi / 208 Allan Stone Galleries, Inc. / 209 Courtesy Robert H. Messing / 212 Roger Malloch, Magnum Photos / 213 John A. Ruge, Copyright © 1969 Saturday Review, Inc. / 214 Wide World Photos / 215 Courtesy Sir Roland Penrose / 216 Robert Doisneau, Rapho Guillumette Pictures / 217 United Press International / 218 Solomon R. Guggenheim Museum / 219 The Museum of Modern Art. Gift of Dominique and John de Menil / 220 University of Kansas Museum of Art / 222 United Press International